RADIO PLAYS

Kevin Gallagher

DOS MADRES

2019

DOS MADRES PRESS INC.
P.O.Box 294, Loveland, Ohio 45140
www.dosmadres.com   editor@dosmadres.com

Dos Madres is dedicated to the belief that the small press is essential to the vitality of contemporary literature as a carrier of the new voice, as well as the older, sometimes forgotten voices of the past. And in an ever more virtual world, to the creation of fine books pleasing to the eye and hand.

Dos Madres is named in honor of Vera Murphy and Libbie Hughes, the "Dos Madres" whose contributions have made this press possible.

Dos Madres Press, Inc. is an Ohio Not For Profit Corporation and a 501 (c) (3) qualified public charity. Contributions are tax deductible.

Executive Editor: Robert J. Murphy

Illustration & Book Design: Elizabeth H. Murphy
www.illusionstudios.net

Typeset in Constantia & SFComic Script Shaded
ISBN 978-1-948017-40-4
Library of Congress Control Number: 2019932029

First Edition

for Estelle

TABLE OF CONTENTS

INTRODUCTION

Radio Plays in Talking Sonnets

These radio poems are 'talking sonnets' in the American grain. While they are 'sonnets' that echo the Italian and to a lesser extent the English versions of the form, they are more analogous to the 'talking blues' of John Lee Hooker, the Reverend Gary Davis, Woody Guthrie, and Bob Dylan. The talking blues brought projective verse to the more formal and imported blues 'ballad' and hit a peak in the late 1950s and early 1960s America. These *Radio Plays* build on the American tradition of John Brooks Wheelwright, Muriel Rukeyser, Ted Berrigan, Bernadette Mayer, Archibald MacLeish, Clark Coolidge, and even a little Robert Lowell.

Only *Gringo Guadalupe* has been read on the radio, but hopefully the publication of this book will lead to more sessions or perhaps some podcasts. I thank Ibbetson Street Press for publishing *Gringo Guadalupe* in chapbook form, *Solstice Literary Magazine* for publishing *Unit and Gray*, and the *Battersea Review* for publishing *God Held My Hand*. I thank, love, and cherish Sean Crehan. Thank you Robert & Elizabeth Murphy for your ears, eyes, and hands. *The Paper Airplane Girls* was written with my daughter, Estelle Sims Gallagher. Our one and only magic marker and Sharpie version of the book is acknowledged and bowed down to. I dedicate this book to Estelle.

FREDDY'S PILGRIMAGE

I.

By the time Blackburn made it to Eugene
his hands were gone and waves had split his planks.

He swam ashore with ol' Welch on his back
as white haired waves chased them with thunder claps.

Now more men in the Pacific-North West
have 'Grace Fears' tattooed on their arms or chests

than all of us in Gloucester combined.
I can see why he 'absolutely had

to go' to Gloucester and see for himself,
though our visiting friends said that all the time.

Grandma was here and could watch the kid.
The three of us slid down the back stairs

from our bungalow up Taylor Court on
Portagee Hill down to the fisherman's nest.

II.

Freddy ran right into an isle of Azoreans
and shouted hey guys I'm a fisherman too!

They started out nice, by ignoring him.
He wouldn't give up and spoke of wooden flakes,

of the *Birdseye* view of salt fish, of kin
stopping Lindsey's attempt to burn it down.

They gave each other the wink, to hit him.
Just before they were all about to swing

Freddy pulled out his cellphone and showed them
pictures of his boat, his nets, and his truck.

The jury was silent for five minutes.
Then the captain shouted he's for real boys!

Soon Freddy and the two of us each had
a parade of tall boy *Bud Lights* in front of us.

III.

The bartender saw another parade that day,
at the *Liberty Tree Mall*, of frosty

sport utility vehicles idling
in an air-conditioned line that started

in front of *Vinny Testa's* and went
way past the shopping carts at the *Target*.

A blue sky was drawn overhead, no clouds.
The revolving doors sparkled new diamonds.

Behind them, a fifteen year old daughter
covered the ring on her belly with one hand,

as she put her other hand on her hip.
You could almost see her comic strip

bubble screaming why does mom have to dress
like that when picking me up from the mall!

You know what they say about you our way?
That the Grand Banks send waves that gallop

on green horses with white manes, Freddy said.
That the boats swing hilariously

between crests and troughs like empty hammocks
in fierce winds.   And the clouds,

the clouds whirl sails that blow away.
And below, below the gill nets hover

the ocean floor like long volleyball nets.
Groundfish try to swim through but get strangled

at the gills. Sometimes the nets detach
from their moorings, and as they drift through

the ocean they keep catching fish.
The nets become heavy then sink

to the floor to be eaten by more groundfish.
Light again, they surface and start over.

V.

Yes. And, is it true that folks out your way
actually think there are Salmon *people*?

That they carefully collect the bones
and lay them into holy little piles

that are then rolled back into the ocean?
That's right, Freddy said, but one guy kept his

and changed the way we do business out there.
A cheek-less Salmon man and a woman

without a chin ripped up out of the sea.
We have never been clear about who had

more fear in us because it is very
hard to ponder without a chin.

The guy shit his pants and threw back the bones,
everyone saved face for plates of food.

VI.

This guy is Tom Cruise with a fucking dimple!
a fisherman said followed by a clash

of amber glasses and a collective laugh.
Yes it *is* Tom Cruise with a fucking dimple!

They didn't even need to hold a vote.
A press conference was immediately assembled:

Tom Cruise with the cutest fucking dimple
in the United States of America,

I've never seen a fisherman with such a face.
What brings you to Gloucester, Massachusetts?!

I'm here visiting my old friend from college,
she works at Harvard and lives up the hill.

"Works at Harvard?!" they collectively gasped.
Moses walked in and took his favorite seat.

Oh missy my dear, the bartender said.
I am so very sorry, if I knew

you worked at Harvard I wouldn't have dared
send the tall boys and whiskey over.

We should be serving white wine to you.
O Charlie, she yelled, can you see if we

have any more Chardonnay in this place?
Freddy was laughing more than they were

when Charlie came running from the basement
with a portable box of "Pink Chablis!?"

Yeah! Pink Chablis for the girl from Harvard!
When I get home no one will believe this.

They surrounded her like a school of fish,
the newest exhibit at the zoo.

VIII.

I'm the only one in the house who works
yet I'm the one who's turning seventy.

Daughter got knocked up when she was fifteen
then the dope that stung her moved right in

once we got the kid back from the state.
Whatever his name is was working

until he got another dame pregnant.
He got depressed and went on welfare

so this girl and the new kid move in too.
On top of all this he's got two dogs

he won't walk so I make them shit out back.
So you think I care when the neighbor calls

to tell me his wife can't stand the dog shit
and that they want to "express their concern"

that they heard someone screaming in my house
last night: "next time I'm going to kill you!"

Lighthouse Taxi, Moses stopped his speech
and covered one ear to talk on the phone.

He gave the bartender back both drinks
and said someone needs a ride downtown.

Let's take Tom Cruise with the fuckin dimple
down to Jazzy Joes and we'll all get laid!

Onward! they said as a loud choir of mates.
We'll roll him in like a wooden decoy

while we hide out behind the tall boy reeds!
No one will understand our secret ploy.

All the girls will think he's Tommy Cruise!
We'll surround the ladies with gill nets,

then send Moses in there with a dory
to pick up the decoy and our catch!

X.

The late evening rain reached Lane's Cove
with the sound of distant crowds

in applause, then became a standing
ovation everywhere. The night sky cleared.

A new mate says look Freddy, a shooting star.
That's no shooting star, Freddy said.

That's God flickin his butts at us.
That Big Dipper ain't no ladle,

it's a battle axe, and now he's got a free hand!
I dunno, choir the guys from the Azores.

we see that as a surrendering flag,
its time to get a room and go to bed.

They all lined up and shook Freddy's hand,
then they said goodbye to their new found friend.

UNIT AND GRAY

PASQUALE

I crossed the Atlantic when I was twelve.
There was nothing to do in Teanu.

Became a conductor of trolley cars—
in uniform, a captain of my ship.

I carried myself well, all the way up
to the *Brown and Sharpe* light bulb factory.

I bought a plot of land, triple-decker,
the first on the block with toilets inside.

A shot of brandy mixed with one raw egg
every morning for most of my life.

I ate the meat during the depression.
I loved your mother but didn't show it.

Milk man, cream on top, skim a bit, ice box.
Every hallway old country crucifix.

ANTOINETTA

I was smart enough to drop out of school
when I was twelve, to take care of my mom.

Much later Louis started to come by.
We would walk and walk all around the block

but he said he would never marry me
until the dam depression was over

and he had a job for a family.
Finally he asked me to marry him.

We went to New York for our honeymoon
then we moved upstairs to the second floor.

My brother Billy did the same next door.
Everyone else was within a few blocks.

I have never read a book in my life.
I will never let my kids get away with that.

NORMA

Masses were in Latin and very long,
though Latin would come in handy in college—

Metamorphoses and biology.
After we finished mouthing 'Our Father'

my brother would say we were rounding third.
Rosary beads, veils, fur coats, white handkerchiefs.

After mass black *Buick Skylark* visits.
First, to swap out the flowers at the graves.

Second, aunts and uncles garlic homes,
stromboli, olives, pizzelles, coffee.

Grandmother sits up: cup, saucer, straight
talking first communions, the old country,

other women, what's for dinner, husbands.
She choked, slumped, then died right in front of me.

PASQUALE TO ETTA

I want to give you a little money.
Please hold on to it just in case

I run into trouble and may need it.
If I don't end up needing it split it

with your brother and sister when I die.
Yes, I am getting married and moving

away with my new wife to Florida.
Yes, she has four kids of her own but I

won't be giving any of them a cent.
She doesn't know anything about it

and you don't know anything about it
and I don't know anything about it.

I ask you to make a promise to me.
Pa! I don't know what you're talkin about!

BILLY TO ANNA

I know you aren't talking to Etta,
so stick your head out the window and talk

to me Anna. I'm down here on the street.
What are you doin down there on the street?!

I'm not going to scream my business
to the whole neighborhood from up here.

Etta says I can't pass the second floor
because you two aren't talking anymore.

She tells me if I'm talking to you
she won't say another word to me too.

Well don't you think she can hear you down there?
She's blasting her radio, she can't hear.

Do you really think I can't hear you two?
You might as well be shouting from the roof!

GIPPI TO ALL THREE

What are you three fightin about?
Uncle Gippi yelled from the first floor porch.

The three of yous leave each other alone.
Shouldn't you be down at Quonset, Billy?

I don't know what we are fighting about
but I'm starting to feel like I should be

thinking about crawling into a hut
over there and just living on the bay

rather than having to guess who's my friend
and who is my enemy every day.

I didn't come back to the family
to watch you all argue about money.

I'm gonna go back to the C.C.C.!
Thirty bucks a month, send some home, keep five.

NORMA AND BILLY JR.

Our parents aren't talking to each other.
Good then let's slip out of the neighborhood

and pretend we are down in New York City.
First we will go over to the *MOMA*,

rooms full of painted American flags,
Giacometti's looking right through me.

Abbott and Costello *Meet the Mummy*
at the *Paramount* on 43rd Street.

Then we'll make our way over to the *Strand*,
pretend to read in Village coffee shops.

Slip away to see the *Basilica*,
hop back on a *Pullman* to Providence.

Have an ice-cream cone on Federal Hill,
then take separate routes back to Unit Street.

II.

Your dad would hear us talking through the screens.
He'd come right over and let himself in

then plop himself in the corner rocker,
unbutton his pants, and light a cigar.

My mom screamed at him 'this isn't your house!
How do you think you can walk right in here?!'

'You're my sister? I lived on top of you
for Chrissakes and my niece is visiting.'

'Etta, Etta, give him a plate of food,'
Louis would say to calm everyone down.

Little pizzas, pickles, antipasta.
Hand-made ravioli and then some ham.

Lady fingers, cannoli, and coffee.
Then 'time to see a man about a horse.'

III.

I have regretted that I didn't go
visit your mother in the hospital.

Our parents weren't talking to each other
and I knew that I would get in trouble.

When she died I just couldn't stop crying.
Well it was much worse when your father died.

My father thought he'd make peace once and for all.
So he walks up to your mom in the hearse

and she starts throwing every curse at him,
wailing her fists and screaming 'how could you?!'

She had enough and willed the cash to use
instead of sharing it as she had said.

We couldn't believe when we got the checks.
All that fighting over ten thousand bucks!

IV.

Today I kneel in front of your casket
and ashes. Your four dogs are at your feet.

Your hands are folded around an icon.
I told my grandkids that you are sleeping,

they asked why you were sleeping in a box.
Of course you are still wearing your glasses.

I know it's you but you don't look like you.
You look like you are wearing a you mask.

A week ago I showed you black and whites.
I wasn't sure if you could see them though.

You looked right at me. You looked right through me.
You squeezed my hand before I had to go.

I stand beside you to shake all their hands.
I can't believe you are there and not here.

MADURO'S MERMAIDS

MAN TALK

Oh my God if I could have just one night
with a fair skinned Venezuelan woman

with big white boobs and with big white booty
I'm the happiest man in Port of Spain

and I won't look at another girl again!
A *Liquid Gold* for him, *Carib* for me,

Kendon said to Justin, ordering beers.
The bar television was showing boats

of Venezuelans fleeing Maduro's
long lines at the grocery store.

They clinked the green bottle to the gold one
then swung around startled in their barstools.

The mermaids are strutting from the ocean!
Justin replied, Your wish just might come true.

I LOVE YOU BABY

Maria Rodriquez walked in with thighs,
calves, hair, and her heels were pumping.

She took her few steps in the bar and stopped
so everyone would look up and see her.

They did but she locked in on our Kendon.
He saw her and started spilling his beer

gaping at a beautiful dream come true.
She walked up to him and said I love you

baby. I've always dreamed of a black man
holding me tight every single night.

Baby I want to get on top of you.
Kendon took her right home and let her do.

She screamed I love you baby I love you.
Kendon screamed marry me I love you too!

WEDDING DAY

Kendon smiled wide as he walked down the aisle,
a big white half moon in a deep black night.

Justin and all his boys bumped their chests
and gave him a wink to brighten his smile.

His mother and friends were rolling their eyes.
Of course she liked that Kendon had a bride

but she really liked Cherelle, his girlfriend.
I don't trust this Maria Rodriquez,

she said and ricocheted a whisper slide
about whether Kendon was a disgrace

or was the luckiest man alive.
What is he going to do with those thighs?

They rode away in a rented limo
with tin cans tied and kicking down the road.

THE CHRISTENING

Baby I'm going back to Caracas
for a little while. My baby sister

just had another baby and I am
not going to miss that girl's baptism.

Of course Maria, family's everything.
Why don't I go back with you and meet them?

Not one of them came back for our wedding.
I want to meet my nieces and nephews.

They're all too poor to come to Trinidad
baby and its not safe for you back home.

I will take pictures and text them to you.
Just thinking about it makes me miss you

already Maria, come home soon.
Don't worry, I'll be back before you know.

NEW NEIGHBORS

They say her real husband's name is Luis.
She came back with him and two fucking kids.

They are living in a flat off St. James.
Things around here will never be the same.

Who is going to tell Kendon she is back?
He hasn't been in the bar in two months.

I haven't seen him at church, or even work.
He thinks she left, she didn't event text.

Kendon's ex-girlfriend Cherelle bangs in bad.
I just saw that Maria who took my man

in the grocery with two kids and her man.
She pulled out a pistol from a paper bag.

I'm gonna kill that Venezuelan bitch
then I'm going over to Kendon's flat!

GOD
HELD MY HAND

o o o o o o o o o o

*Argentina was ruled by a dictatorship from 1976 to
1983. Under the regime, approximately 30,000 people
"disappeared". In July of 2012, when the poet was
living in Buenos Aires, two former presidents were
convicted for overseeing the abduction of 500 babies
who were taken at birth and given to supporters of
the dictatorship after their rightful mothers were
killed. Now the 'children of the disappeared' are
learning their true identities. One of the presidents,
Jorge Rafael Videla, said "God held my hand" during
the country's dirty war. In 2016, the government of
Argentina authorized itself to obtain DNA samples
from individuals suspected to have been abducted
and has particularly targeted the heirs to Clarin,
a newspaper that supported the dictatorship and
continues to publish to this day.*

o o o o o o o o o o

GENERAL

I.

At least thirty in this school will be due,
for them there is another set of rules.

We use the kitchen table for the births,
these bitches need to be worth something first.

Then we send them to the skies to pay
for what they've done. But their children stay.

The bastard kids are there for the taking.
There is a long line of soldiers waiting.

The mothers dive into the River Plate,
the children are born to accept their fate.

The two of us are just doing our job.
Just remember they were going to rob

what we took from them first for good reason.
Save the kids. Kill the women for treason.

I don't know how to deliver a child
so keep some women around for a while

and make sure they don't make a bloody mess.
If they cross you say do what the soldier says

and there is a chance we will keep you alive--
at least to deliver another child.

But you may have to hold the mother's hand
then scream she should push as hard as she can.

She may bleed too much. Don't look in her eyes.
No matter to us if she lives or dies.

We have strict orders to keep the children.
We don't care about communist women.

Do let me know if you yourself want one.
I can find you an heir, a long lost son.

III.

This isn't going as well as we planned.
They are obeying all of our commands:

deliver your babies as fast as you can.
We fill them with drugs, we load them in vans,

we pile them alive in helicopters,
we throw them out when we get our orders.

The bodies spin to the river like fans,
falling from our aircraft 'like little ants.'

But instead of sinking to the bottom
of the River Plata where we dropped them

they are washing up on the river bank.
I am afraid that we have been outflanked.

Just slit open their stomachs beforehand.
They'll fill with water, and sink with god's hand.

CHORUS

They got to play god with all of our lives
but that god didn't get the final say.
It's hard to find out your life is a lie.

Thrown from helicopters in the sky
then washed on the banks of the River Plate.
They got to play god with all our lives.

Decided who lived, decided who died.
So we cried and marched every Thursday.
It's hard to find out your life is a lie.

That is what motivated us to try.
That is what motivated us to pray.
They tried to play god with all our lives

but we knew our god would answer our cries.
We knew we'd hold our grandchildren one day.
It's hard to find out your life is a lie.

We're here for you now, your hands are untied.
Let us go forward and be on our way.
They tried to play god with all of our lives.
It's hard to find out your life is a lie.

ABUELA

I.

I finally found my daughter on my
television set, diving black and white

like a little bomb breaking the river
high from a hovering helicopter.

My little angel disappeared six months ago.
She had just told me the news on the phone.

She was going to bring us all a new child.
She said it was time to extend our line,

to love against the dying of the light.
Love and a child are the best way to fight.

She saw how sacred it could be for love
to be the source of making another

little soul to help save us from this place.
I close my eyes but I still see her face.

Father you have to help us find the child!
How am I supposed to live my life while

I know my daughter was dropped from the skies?
I know my grand daughter is still alive.

My husband said not to tell anyone.
Every time the doorbell rings he thinks they've come.

My husband doesn't want to die that way
but we can't just sit around here and pray.

It is they who are trying to play god.
You have to assure me that the good lord

will save their souls and give him back to me.
He is in prison and he must go free.

This is a photo of whom I must find.
I won't stop looking for him until I die.

I don't want to see a green Ford Falcon
coming down my street. I cannot fathom

what those men with no minds will do to me.
We fear we can't be what we want to be.

We stay in the house, we pull back the blinds,
and think of other things to do with our time.

Sometimes the blood makes us spill on the street
but there is nothing we can do to compete

with the tear gas, tanks, and brutal force.
For every death there is less remorse.

Rape is no different than a cigarette.
The only thing this junta regrets

is that sometimes we make them get home late.
When they kiss their wives do they see my face?

IV.

They underestimated our march that goes
every Thursday to the Plaza de Mayo.

We plant placard trees with each child's face.
We have built a file on every case.

We parade each week, we continue praying.
They continue rounding up and slaying,

though now we know where each soldier lives.
We won't give up until each of them gives

each of us all of our grandchildren back.
We have disguised ourselves as maids to crack

into your homes, identify our babies,
and start calling them out by their real names!

When it is time to come back from the playground
empty strollers are all that will be found.

CHORUS

They got to play god with all of our lives
but that god didn't get the final say.
It's hard to find out your life is a lie.

Thrown from helicopters in the sky
then washed on the banks of the River Plate.
They got to play god with all our lives.

Decided who lived, decided who died.
So we cried and marched every Thursday.
It's hard to find out your life is a lie.

That is what motivated us to try.
That is what motivated us to pray.
They tried to play god with all our lives

but we knew our god would answer our cries.
We knew we'd hold our grandchildren one day.
It's hard to find out your life is a lie.

We're here for you now, your hands are untied.
Let us go forward and be on our way.
They tried to play god with all of our lives.
It's hard to find out your life is a lie.

DISAPPEARED

I.

I saw their faces every morning.
The final page of *Pagina 12*

made me wonder if I resembled them.
I felt like I didn't have any friends

because I didn't dare say anything
to anyone who might suggest I ring

the place where they sample your DNA.
How could I go home and what would I say?

You loved me, raised me, you put me through school
but now I know you've played me for a fool.

I'm leaving you now, I'll never come back!
I just couldn't think about doing that.

Yet I couldn't go a day without that page.
Now I go for the eyes in every face.

I had just dropped my daughter off at school.
A woman came to me and said you will

find this very hard to take, I'm afraid
I may be your grand mother. Go away!

I screamed at her, she cowered to the ground.
She said that is how her son-in-law would sound

when he was raging against the regime.
I said what you are saying is obscene.

I lived with my family all of my life.
Its been ten years since my grandmother died.

She said I knew this would be hard to take.
Believe me this is nothing I can fake.

I've been searching for you for thirty years.
I looked in her eyes and saw mine in hers.

III.

Now my kids call me by a different name.
I say nothing will ever be the same.

Your grandparents have been living a lie
and I don't know what to make of my life.

For thirty years I ate at their table.
Those two people are those that enabled

me to be the person I have become.
Now my constitution has become undone.

Now am I supposed to send them to jail?
If I don't what I am supposed to tell

my grandmother who has found the real me?
The answer is pretty easy to see.

I will send them to jail to do what's right.
Today is the first day of my new life.

MADRE?

I never had any hate towards him.
I loved him as if he was my own kin.

I stayed home every time he was sick.
I would stay up all night beside his crib.

I taught him to see what was right and wrong.
I taught him how to read, write, and sing songs.

I drove him to go on all of his dates.
I begged for him not to make no mistakes.

I fed him I bathed him I clothed him too.
I don't know what this world is coming to.

I pick out a child. I give him a life.
I serve my country. I am a good wife.

I wouldn't have done this if I had known.
I raised this child, only to be disowned.

CHORUS

They got to play god with all of our lives
but that god didn't get the final say.
It's hard to find out your life is a lie.

Thrown from helicopters in the sky
then washed on the banks of the River Plate.
They got to play god with all our lives.

Decided who lived, decided who died.
So we cried and marched every Thursday.
It's hard to find out your life is a lie.

That is what motivated us to try.
That is what motivated us to pray.
They tried to play god with all our lives

but we knew our god would answer our cries.
We knew we'd hold our grandchildren one day.
It's hard to find out your life is a lie.

We're here for you now, your hands are untied.
Let us go forward and be on our way.
They tried to play god with all of our lives.
It's hard to find out your life is a lie.

POLICE

We need a sample from every one.
Anyone out there could be a lost son,

a lost daughter, grandson, or granddaughter.
We must be guided by the grandmothers

who kept this alive every Thursday.
Everyone must obey or have to pay.

Collective memory is on the line.
The country must move on to better times.

The family is usually gone
sometime around ten. When breakfast is done

they go clean then pile in cars for *Clarin*.
If we want to be sure we aren't a scene

we should raid the house precisely at noon.
Let's make sure our watches are in tune.

DISAPPEARED?

I came home from work to a disaster.
Everything we owned has been passed over

and turned upside down without any care,
until they found my drawer of underwear.

That's all they needed to get their sample.
A sample is all they need for ample

evidence to frame me and my brother.
How will either of us every recover?

I know I was adopted fair and square.
Yes in the past my parents were unfair

but they wouldn't go on trial for that.
You want to pin them with the entire past!

Protection of privacy is vital.
I haven't disappeared and that is final!

CHORUS

They got to play god with all of our lives
but that god didn't get the final say.
It's hard to find out your life is a lie.

Thrown from helicopters in the sky
then washed on the banks of the River Plate.
They got to play god with all our lives.

Decided who lived, decided who died.
So we cried and marched every Thursday.
It's hard to find out your life is a lie.

That is what motivated us to try.
That is what motivated us to pray.
They tried to play god with all our lives

but we knew our god would answer our cries.
We knew we'd hold our grandchildren one day.
It's hard to find out your life is a lie.

We're here for you now, your hands are untied.
Let us go forward and be on our way.
They tried to play god with all of our lives.
It's hard to find out your life is a lie.

POST SCRIPT: ON A SUNDAY IN PALERMO

Pesos dive
as dollars fly

north to 'safety'.
Empty restaurants

in Villa 15 & 31
en Constitucion.

Café at home
comida y almuerzo too.

Just one Malbec
out at night

so you don't
have to turn

on your lights.
Sell the car

take the bus
and walk

to work
to church

to the market
to the park

for a date
or watch TV.

Sunday in Palermo
the wait

was one hour
rather than two.

Malbec flows
like blood.

Glasses cling
like light little bells.

If you have
@real dollar

2 bottles of Malbec
5 Ojos de bife

and an ensalada
for just $70 US.

Pot holes
on Libertador

stretch yawns.
Hub caps roll

like escaping coins.
The roots

of old Tilo trees
break loose

from the sidewalks
like Zombies

bursting
from their graves.

COME OVER AND HELP US

I.

Is there anything that no one can steal
under Roman numerals that reveal

a triple extra-large in the balance
making you fall in and follow in a trance

that trades in the tarot for credit cards
to get everything you ever wanted

except first class tickets to Andean trails
never to be found no electric stairs

and the air thinner than the splitting hairs
that separate the circus from the fair?

In each case you let the elephants out
to cut their tusks and wiggle about

the fact you were both happy in a cage
red handed, pants down, lights out on the stage

II.

There's nothing more I want to be than you
so you can get plates of fossil fuel food

gallop on the strongest horse with a flag
and your pocket book will never get snagged

my opportunities in life are few
and so many fortunes are ready made

so there's only one thing for us to do
but it will not be written down or said

I'm sorry I turned the tables on you
you were hard to look at when you were dead

you need more than math to derive those roots
love doesn't have to be made in a bed

and I wanted to go sleep in the cave
since I'd seen the light I thought I'd be saved

III.

Once I had some all I wanted was more
so I had to rob the entire store

but after I ran out onto the street
I became drenched with rain, pelted with sleet

so I realized I had to dry the place
by sucking up the entire sea

until it made balloons out of my face
that lifted me above forests and trees

so I could look down at it all and see
that all of it had to be mine, all mine

fly like a butterfly sting like a bee
I'll punch you in the face a thousand times

don't give me all this be all you can be
I pity the fool that's chicken to die

IV.

O who are you calling to when you rhyme
your pentameter is your greatest vice

now the words come down from the times
they arrange themselves as if you had met

just so you could finish the longest line
with a design that no one could forget

without a room for ambitious regrets
from a wonderful one where we can dine

and chandeliers swing like the pendulums
that go back and forth under all the clocks

that tell each one of us the time and send
the wind to wrap our ships around the rocks

for the bronze lady with her child in cloth
for the Mary with her boat that you mock

V.

Whenever I'm alone I think of you
it gets harder the further I'm away

to spin the blood and make the bones decay
while working inside the heart attack looms

so I somersault like a circus fool
lay out a chess game and ask you to play

but you say I don't like to play that way
you stupid cue ball in a game of pool

that thinks you can play against all the rules
take me the way you want without my say

you know you look pathetic when you drool
your eyes get wide, tongue out and your cheeks cave

love can change if there is another day
if you want to love me you need to pray

VI.

You are not making love you're expecting rain
even a Robin Hood disguise can't help

a happy hobo jumps on a train
you are letting it known you have to yell

the kerosene from the insurance men
blazes loud as you laugh with all of them

screaming I think I can I think I can
but you know they will run out of gas

so now is the time to put on your mask
and hide under the bridge with the trolls

it's easy for you to step up to the task
blow dynamite for the heads to roll

it's amazing that some people moan
when so many hearts are open and roar

VII.

I should have stood and whispered to the dove
but I couldn't do it without crying

I let bullshit stand in front of my pride
now I don't recognize what has become

of the fact you want to clock me in the face
because I didn't look inside your eyes

and realize there was a time and place
to put ribbons and double knotted ties

around the neck of every single lie
and not have to talk about every lace

not to have every oyster shell pried
for a pearl in a snapping velvet case

that gets opened to French hook from your ear
that sets me aside from all my peers

VIII.

There's no such thing as the back of the bus
and in Gloucester we say in cod we trust

because Ben Franklin got the Atlantic
in negotiations with the British

Richard Pryor said justice was 'just us'
and we can never forget Atticus

every time we think there is a landslide
we stand up and do what it is we must

Nelson Mandela Roxbury parade
Vaclav Havel on a velvet tirade

Gloria Steinem a spade is a spade
Prince is wearing a raspberry beret

just look at all this history we made
while leaving some of the future behind

IX.

I make sure all the banks have a lever
and that all the mattresses have a pea

weathermen don't know about the weather
wisdom fights with our curiosities

the hedge funds are trying to be clever
they think they know what none of us can see

at the end of the day they have no show
you can sit through without a handkerchief

lines between risk and hope have to sever
when trying to be safe but also free

we cannot count on angels to hover
in our sunny world of uncertainty

there's only one way to guard the safe
let no one inside or out of this place

X.

There are some grapes that carry too much weight
don't even try bringing them up the stairs

just put them in the bowl on the table
next to a candle, a knife, and two pears

then look at them without moving for hours
can you sit there without taking a bite?

even though you know the grapes aren't sour
and the candle can get you through the night

easy if you are separate places
and neither of them has a fork or spoon

you can spend the entire night pacing
even if there is no light under the moon

patience means that you are never waiting
deep into the pool but really wading

XI.

I love that courage is your favorite word
and the last thing you are is a lion

you see beauty in the movement of herds
but you are never with the flocks flying

because standing still has its own reward
although the ties it has are not binding

nothing is spinning faster than our world
the only thing worse is the unwinding

you may be surrounded by men in capes
and smiles inviting you to funerals

that cannot be found in the basement tapes
or from the oyster's mouth spitting out pearls

stand up to the devil and to the lord
don't be moved, unscrew the locks from the doors

XII.

You will never let me be a coward
I know you will be there when I mess up

from one bloom can come a thousand flowers
each one of them powdered with pollen on top

so when we sneeze all the seeds are released
and new Bethlehems everywhere are born

scores of children on a mission for peace
and to let it be known we have been warned

if we don't close our eyes we cannot see
all the punctuation we need to live

in a way that allows us all to breathe
in a way you can continue to give

no you don't have to get down on your knees
we've locked the door and thrown away the key

O yes the world is a beautiful place
to be born in to if you dance with the grace

and fortitude the way you're supposed to
along the routes that have been laid for you

you can swing from the ropes of the captain's tower
even though the ocean is so damn deep

you know you can swim and land on your feet
no one said you didn't have the power

you must try to get to the other side
close your eyes you will know what it looks like

you believe you can swim against the tide
because the golden key is on the kite

that will enable the future to be bright
and light up eternities of nights

XIV.

I promise to be your friend forever
if we met now what is the time of day?

when I say always you will say never
one of us does, the other doesn't pray

you say that you will laugh at all my jokes
you say that all my ideas are genius

O you are throwing me more and more rope
but it won't become untied between us

because I always shoot through golden hoops
that hang over my head every day

yes the angels have taught me how to stoop
down almost touching the ground for no pay

the laughing can sound like it's own reward
but this cane is mightier than your sword

XV.

Sunlight and your interior lamp is on
a drama of overlapping densities

the garrison is packed with soldier songs
shields of garbage can lid dreams and fees

the linens on the clotheslines are sailing strong
vanishing points antagonize what we see

there is a chance that we have this all wrong
but wait there is another place to be

the clouds are whiffs from smoking gongs
but nobody dares to call the police

newly made flags map the front of the barn
circles of parades with the waving trees

a place for value in a world alarmed
a revelation of continuity and free

FREDDY'S SHORTS

WHERE IS WHEELIE WHEN YOU NEED HIM?

Freddy and his friend Sean took their *Big Wheels*
to the top of Charles Drive then let go.

Yeah, we were *Wheelie and the Chopper Bunch*.
Fred called that he was *Revs*, Sean was *Scrambles*.

When they hit the turn off at the bottom
they dropped their *Chuck Taylors, Fred Flinstone* style—

wearing out their plastic wheels and rubber souls
as they fish-tailed wide around the corner.

Then Brett Lange would spin out of his driveway
saying 'I'm *Chopper*' on his *Green Machine*.

Muffle it! Don't try to run us off
the road *Chopper*, you won't like how it ends!

Brett rammed into *Revs* and broke his *Big Wheel*.
Scramble screamed out 'I told ya! I told ya!

GROUNDED AGAIN

Freddy was eyeing that banana seat
all weekend long then his Uncle let him

take it home if it was okay with mom.
Fred's dad had the fun job of fitting

the entire bike in the already stuffed
77 aqua blue *Vega*

hatchback with an aluminum engine.
Freddy fell asleep on the long ride home.

Next thing he knew he was off to church
in green plaid *Toughskins* and a pair of *Keds*.

Fred begged the whole ride back to ride the bike.
'After you change out of your Sunday clothes'

was the last thing he heard before crashing
into the mailbox and ripping his pants.

EVACUATION GAME

Freddy was loving that he batted lefty.
He had a stance between a Rod Carew

and Cecil Cooper during the *Brewer* years.
Rob Barry would pitch him high and inside

Pittsburgh Pirate Kent Tekulve sidearm style.
He'd snap Rob's hairless tennis ball curve

and jump and wave it fair like Carlton Fisk--
up and over Hilton Kaderli's fence.

Hilton's wife would run to her porch, perfect hair,
hands on hips, and hurl her southern accent

right back over the fence in a manner
that scared the shit out of Robby Bourgeois.

'Don't you hit your balls in my garden boys!'
But by then we'd already disappeared.

LUIS TIANT FAN CLUB ALUM

Although Freddy will always be sour
that his sister went and traded his Topps

Ted Williams and Roberto Clemente
for a box of stupid match-box cars,

he still fondly remembers having
a hot dog and a beer every inning

every Sunday he could at *Fenway Park*
from seventy-five to eighty-five.

After warming up for a few innings
he'd stand in the middle of the row

and scream "Dominos!" then laugh as they
let him by to get another pair.

FREDDY'S SMOKIN

After Freddy got in another fight
with David Cawthon he decided to

go back home and lay on the couch all day
with *Tales from Topographic Oceans* on.

How could David dare to say John Paul Jones
was even comparable to Chris Squire?

In those days words like that were worse than war
but Freddy was in a give peace a chance

period so he did a few bong hits
and got lost in the underwater world

of another Roger Dean album cover.
His Panasonic could stack two thirty-threes

so he only had to flip the vinyl
every forty minutes, rather than twenty.

WRECKER

Freddy could dribble like no one's business.
No one could take the ball away from him.

Except of course for his coach, Peterson.
The coach benched Freddy for breaking training.

Sure Freddy and his pals puffed some rockets
and listened to the *Legion of Mary*

on the way to practice at *Henry James*,
But it never affected Freddy's game.

So the scouts from the big college teams left
looking for other kids with feet like Fred.

Freddy went off to Boulder with the *Dead*
and it finally affected his game.

That's why Freddy got pissed off when he read
that Coach P got busted snorting cocaine.

FREDDY LAYS IT DOWN

Hey why are you swinging on your hammock
with that BB gun and smiling Freddy?

Because I bought this brand new bird feeder,
it is supposed to bring woodpeckers in flocks!

What does that have to do with all the shots
that are flying around the neighborhood?

Some neighbors say they've even seen blood.
What's going on around here Freddy? Talk!

You suppose I'll get a word in edgewise
when you're carrying on yappin like that?

You'll scare away woodpeckers with those cries!
 I'm shootin the stupid pigeons that flap

over here trying to get a free ride.
They come, ping, like water balloons, they splat!

COMPOSITION IN BLUE, NOIR, ET ROUGE

Freddy went to New York City to see
the big Piet Mondrian exhibit.

It was his wife's idea but he loved it.
"There's no better place I'd rather be!"
he assured her.
                    She was worried that he
was wearing a smile but having a fit.

It had been years since she had seen him sit
in front of anything but a TV
for more than fifteen minutes.
                    But he sat
in front of the same forty inch painting
for the whole afternoon.
                    She thought, "what
in heaven's name is that man thinking?"

He later remarked that he felt right at
home that day. "It was like I was watching
a game and the emergency station
identification colors popped on."

FREDDY'S CUT

Freddy went to Ricardo's Barbershop
on Huntington Avenue and he screamed

Ricky make me look like Dino Radja!
I am not no Eric Montross sidekick.

Make me look like Dino and I will glide
like Clyde Drexler. I will drive like Tiny,

and I will shoot the three like a white Ray.
Ricardo turn me into a Dino!

If you do they'll be asking 'what's the buzz
tell me what's a happenin' like Jesus

Christ Superstar back in the seventies.
Ricardo I will do my own commercials:

If you want to look like you're NBA,
Get yourself underneath Ricardo's blade!

FREDDY TO THE END ZONE

How could Freddy turn down five hundred bucks
an hour to tutor a Saudi Prince?

Freddy just had to turn up at the Ritz &
go over English and Math with the kid.

So what if sometimes Fred waited four hours.
He'd gaze at the Prince's Super Bowl tix.

The Prince would boast he went to every game
since the Refrigerator Bear in eighty-five.

Then there were Shaq's big kicks in the glass case.
Oh yeah, and when Fred waited he got paid!

Then one night the Prince ruined the whole game.
Fred said write this paper over again.

I have no time, I'll give you twenty-five grand.
That was the hardest door Freddy ever slammed.

GALITEA AND HER PYG

Fred made "his doll" into the perfect catch.
He cast her with a permanent smile.
At parties she laughed at just the right times.

He'd boast, "She was just an egg about to hatch.
I took her in and sculpted her from scratch.
Look at her now! There's no better prize!"

To his credit, she pleased everyone's eyes.
To his proud arm, she was always attached.

But no, he hardly ever let her speak.
"Women this pretty don't have minds," he'd say.

But one evening when he was fast asleep,
she lipsticked a note on the window shade.

When he woke he rubbed his eyes to read:
"I'm sick of your shit! I leave with your face."

GRINGO GUADALUPE

JOE BEGINS

Everything's too expensive to be poor.
In this world I can never have enough.
I feel like I can't get my head above
water. But, we won't worry anymore.

All heads will turn when I walk through the door.
They'll say, "Now that guy really has his stuff
together. Check out his new car. He must
not have a worry in the entire world."

I'll come back in a couple of weeks.
I'll test the waters down in Mexico.
We'll leave soon after I get back, so please
start thinking about what stays and what goes.

Of course I'll hate what you want to keep.
Of course you'll love what I want to go.

AT THE COMPANY ORIENTATION IN MEXICO

We like all of our employees to have wives.
They keep a man as calm as he can be.
The single man has nights that are just too free.
They're always putting their time before our time.

Remember that it's our ladder you climb,
and it leads to what you can't yet see.
Most importantly, you must believe
in everything the company designs.

There is one town where the employees live.
It has a school where teachers speak English.
The shopping mall is fully equipped with
TVs and burgers—whatever you wish.

And that is what we are willing to give.
A perfect place for you and the misses.

ANGEL IN HER FATHER'S SLEEP

Your daughter tracked the star of Bethlehem.
She stood by the manger and watched him lie.
Now she will give birth to the son again.

So when I'm finished wake up all your friends.
Tell them we have Mary before our eyes.
Your daughter tracked the star of Bethlehem.

Your daughter's alive! She's been heaven sent.
You are the luckiest father in time!
Your daughter will carry the sun again.

From all over the earth people will come
to see her face, enlightened and divine.
Your daughter tracked the star of Bethlehem.

Tell all the poets to ink their pens.
Now is the time to finish the longest line.
Yes, she will give birth to the son again.

Mary's stronger than she's ever been.
Laughter and love will replace the world's cries.
Your daughter tracked the star of Bethlehem.
Now she will give birth to the son again.

FATHER AWAKE

An angel came to me in last night's sleep
and blessed me with a truth that wets my eyes.
I cry with all the rain inside the sky.
The earth spins, but from your womb Christ will creep

into our world and save us all in one sweep.
I'm so happy I think I could fly
around the earth ten times and not be tired.

Bring me Satan! I want to see him weep!

He thought this century was his to burn.
Just when you think they're fixed the tables turn.
Now there is love for all ten times over!

Oh, loving God, thanks for my little girl.
My little girl was born to save the world!

AT THE DOORBELL

All that I need in my life is my son.
If my boy dies I will die behind him.
This poor little boy's life has just begun

to make sense to him. He just learned to run
and chase the butterflies and robins.
All that I need in my life is my son.

I pray for him before each day is done.
I beg you Mary, make him breathe again.
This poor little boy's life has just begun.

The angel's news is brighter than the sun.
You are the messenger that God has sent.
All that I need in my life is my son.

Unlike Abraham he's my only one.
Do not let him die, it is I who has sinned.
This poor little boy's life has just begun.

I know that he is destined to become
better than anything that I have been.
All that I need in my life is my son.
This poor little boy's life has just begun.

AS THE NEIGHBORS WATCH
FROM THE PORCHES

Here she did what any human would do,
she held the boy in her arms and she cried.
(If her husband was there he would have died!)
At that point the crowd had no doubts, they knew,

Mary was back and she looked like me or you.
At first none of them could believe their eyes;
but this was not a Mary in disguise,
centuries of prayer had sharpened their view.

The boy's eyes were widest, he cried out "Mom."
All you could hear was her heart and her veins.
She stood there with the child under her arms,
she felt as if she didn't need a brain.

Believe me, no one here's putting you on.
Then everyone around knew her name.

MARY TO THE CROWD

Everything is with me, yes I am
the sun through the trees, history and the soil.
I will bear a son that will rule this land.

I am the sharp ax, the force, and the lamb.
My blood hung like roses over your doors.
Everything is with me, yes I am

the iambs of all tongues and grains of sand
cracked from the hourglass to be castle toys.
I will bear a son that will rule this land.

He'll stand atop mountains that have spanned
the centuries waiting to hear his voice.
Everything is with me, yes I am

echoing with atoms, heat and a fan;
cooling the plants, hearts and everything's noise.
I will bear a son that will rule this land.

It's all right here in the palm of my hand,
where its been all mapped out, I have no choice.
Everything is with me, yes, I AM.
I will bear a son that will rule this land.

DO YOU BELIEVE IN MIRACLES?

Of course their crying babies made her cry.
How was she to hug all of them?
Her yard sprouted a mushroom field of tents.
She decided to go one at a time.

A woman down the block had doubting eyes;
as she watched Mary on television
her son coughed over and over again.
To her, her neighbor was a lie.

He hadn't opened up his eyes for days
but when she turned the TV off he yelled
"take me to Mary mom! Take me today!"

Of course she knew it was Mary he felt,
she held him tight and they were on their way.

CASUAL DAY

Your wife's making the company look bad.
She's in newspapers all over the world.
I thought you said she's just a little girl.
She's the biggest thing, she's a Jesus fad!

The people at the top are getting mad.
Since we globalized the entire firm,
nothing has ever caused this kind of stir.
You're blowing all chances you could have had.

Our Mexico could be your new frontier.
If the Mexicans find out about this
you'll be on the next train out of here.

I advise you to go home with the fear
of me in you, hold her tight with your fists.

Marriage is the car that the husband steers.

THROUGH A PARTING OF THE CROWDS

I didn't believe anything they said.
If a neighbor's not a bitch she's a god.
Are they wrong? Place your hands on my son's head

and prevent my kid from joining the dead
and I'll believe! I'll even quit my job.
I never believe anything they say

but if you tell me you're Mary instead;
I will follow you with a bowl and starve!
Save my son's life, place your hands on his head.

He's spent the last six weeks lying in bed.
Show us your love Mary. Silence his cough!
I didn't believe anything they said

but my son called your name again and again.
I am finding all of this a bit odd.
I ask that you place your hands on his head,

cure him, then begin with all the world's dreads.
Then my son and I will join the applause.
I didn't believe anything they said
but I will, place your hands on his head.

WHAT GOES UP ...

Mary smiled and raised her hands in the air.
The surrounding crowd immediately knelt.

The sun behind her began to set
and became a halo on the horizon;
flaring Mary into what the crowd saw
as a beaming gold cross hovering above the ground.

The poor little boy never coughed again.
When Mary stretched out her hand the boy cried.
His voice was the only sound in the sky.

All the reporters stood arched with their pens,
this was perfect, their deadline was at ten.

When Mary took him in her arms he died.

The light went out in everyone's eyes.
Most of them would never have faith again.

THE PAPER AIRPLANE GIRLS

with Estelle Sims Gallagher

FRIENDS NO MORE

Hannah and Petra were the best of friends.
They walked to school together every day

and sat right next to each other in class.
They always ate at the same lunch table

and were inseparable at recess.
They were on the same soccer team, carpooled

to the same weekend lessons and activities
and were the leaders of the Girl Scout troop.

One day after a silly argument
their parents said they wouldn't speak again.

And because the parents were not speaking
the only thing the parents agreed on:

You can not play with Hannah again!
You can not play with Petra again!

I LOCK MY DOOR

Hannah went up to her room and she cried
so hard she had bubbles in her eyes

that made her see a blurry inner world
through the pane of a locked up little girl.

Her window was open and the summer wind
opened her drapes and gave her measure

to wipe her eyes and look at the real sky—
so much more clear than the sky in her mind.

She could see Petra's window right next door.
How could she not talk to her anymore?

Without Petra life is a complete bore.
I'll never leave this room. I lock my door!

To both our parents I declare war!
Then, a paper airplane landed on her floor.

LETTER #1

from Petra

Our parents say our friendship has to end
even though we don't know why they are fighting.
I promise that I will always be your friend.

When I go to my room I will send
you a note in an airplane each night.
Our parents say our friendship has to end

but we can still be friends. I know we can.
We'll just keep our friendship out of their sight.
I promise that I will always be your friend

even if sometimes I have to pretend
that I haven't seen you in my whole life.
Our parents say our friendship has to end.

Our planes can make our friendship of the wind.
Our planes carry our friendship when in flight.
I promise that I will always be your friend.

I promise over and over again
that someday our parents will see the light.

Our parents say our friendship has to end.
I promise that I will always be your friend.

FLYING IN A PAPER AIRPLANE

By the time she finished Petra's letter
a huge smile swung across Hannah's face.

There's no way her parents can catch her
when she is flying in a paper airplane.

She won't be seen playing with Petra
and they would never be in the same place.

She grabbed some paper and got on her knees
then folded the paper in half and then she

re-opened it to fold in the corners
twice and then fold each of the sides back in half.

She made a paper airplane that could fly
against her parent's wishes with the winds!

Then she unfolded it to a blank page,
took out her crayons and began to write.

LETTER #2

from Hannah

You are my best friend in the entire world.
I thought I would cry for the rest of my life.
Let's call ourselves *The Paper Airplane Girls*.

We can fly the skies together and turn
pages of notebooks into planes that fly.
You are my best friend in the entire world.

Thank you for your letter that you hurled
in my window as I cried through the night.
Let's call ourselves *The Paper Airplane Girls*.

Writing letters to each other can cure
the ban that our parents put on our lives.
You are my best friend in the entire world.

We are next door neighbors and we are girls
that love each other while our parents fight.
From now on we are *The Paper Airplane Girls*

that know truths that even parents can't learn.
Our friendship is what holds us together tight.

You are my best friend in the entire world.
From now on we are *The Paper Airplane Girls*.

LETTER #3

from Petra

I have a secret plan for us to play.
Hannah isn't your birthday coming soon?
Say you want a costume party birthday

party this year and you want us all to stay
late—but we cannot take off our costumes.
That is my secret plan for us to play

with each other. I think I can sway
my mother to think I'm crying in my room.
Say you want a costume party birthday,

my costume will never give me away.
I'll be a witch that doesn't fly a broom.
We have a secret plan so we can play.

A flying witch in a paper airplane
that will pop all the birthday balloons!
Say you want a costume party birthday.

Say you will not have it any other way.
This may be the only way I see you.

We have a secret plan for us to play.
We want to have a costume party birthday.

THE COSTUME PARTY

Among her guests was a disco diva,
a *Scooby-doo*, a *Statue of Liberty*,

and last but not least *Fancy Nancy*.
Nancy decided that she would be mean

and started poking fun at the birthday girl
for having a plain vanilla costume

and for spending all her life in her room.
Fancy Nancy made the birthday girl cry.

A witch came swooping in on her airplane
and told the girl that she better go home.

Hannah's mother hugged the young witch
then lifted the mask to give her a kiss.

She screamed "Petra what are you doing here?!"
Then smiled and thanked her for being a friend.

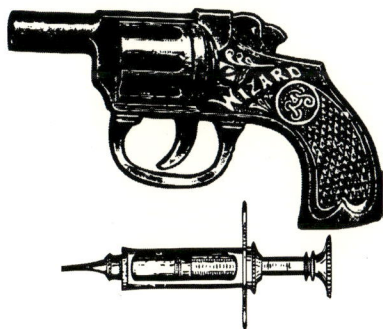

BIG BILLY
AND
LITTLE BILLY

I

Big Billy started snorting heroin
four short months ago. "It was my wife's fault."
At that time the two had just left the vault
and decided they wanted out, not in.

She started with a ten bag every alternate
week or so –a start that wouldn't halt.
Big Billy wouldn't touch the stuff. Not him.

He opened up his own furniture store;
buying, selling, and delivering fine
and not so fine clocks, chairs, or just drawers.

He learned freedom could be a good time.

His wife soon found it an enormous bore
and moved to starting each day with a dime.

Little Billy, their son, wanted to be
just like Big Billy, but he was too young.

Most of the time that didn't stop him.
Big Billy said he couldn't believe
what a cheap bastard his friend had become.

When that friend came by the store to buy some
chairs, "The cheap bastard's over here dad, see?"
Little Billy jeered, his chin high and his chest out.

Big Billy hated that he had to give
away the chair for such a slip. But the pout
that poor little Billy's face had to live
with would prove not to affect Big Billy's clout.
In fact, it eased Big Billy to forgive.

III.

A month later they were doing a bundle
a day together. That is four of those
little dime bags (forty bucks) up the nose.

Now, if you or I snorted just one
of those little bags we would be so done
we'd be in the morgue with tags on our toes!
But junkies build tolerance with each dose.
Big Billy and his wife had just begun.

Forty bucks a day wasn't tough for them.
The furniture store was doing quite well.

The rent in Allston was cheap, and by then
business was so good Big Billy could sell
somebody a table and couch for their den
and steal their China through the back stairwell.

IV.

More and more people started coming by
looking for things that got lost on the day
Big Billy delivered them something. Hey
that mahogany desk over there is mine
they'd say.
        Big Billy, although stoned, could lie:

Yeah, you wish you had the money to pay
for a desk as nice as this one he'd say.
I bought this in Essex, you must be blind!

Somehow they would eventually go
away. For moments, Big Billy had won.

But each day would become more and more slow.
So slow Big Billy bought himself a gun.

No big deal when numb from head to toe.
For target practice he'd shoot at the sun.

V.

Last week Little Billy saw Big Billy
snort three whole bags of smack in the back room.

Gee daddy your face looks like a full moon.
Will Little Billy be like that, will he?

Come now Little Billy don't be so silly.
If you want to be like me you're a fool.
This big boy medicine's not for you.

Why dad, will big boy medicine hurt me?
Yes Little Billy, you are only seven years old!

But I will be able to have a gun!

At that point Big Billy's body went cold,
He saw what was happening and was stunned.

As Big Billy's face started to unfold
he mumbled my boy will never have one.

THE LOVE SONG
OF
FREDDY SAPIENZA

I.

His trophies: four walls of **KISS** picture disks;
a black and white Robert Plant lemon shot;
a life size Larry Bird--you could measure
your life by height; and Freddy's waterbed.

At thirty he left it all behind, a shrine
to the *Helter Skelter* double feature,
to *Batman and Robin*, to the *Monkees*,
and to the girl who lived across the street.

Talking to truck drivers on their CBs,
traded for a mother of a lover.
Yes Freddy left all that for the women.
She would be taken away, sorta, twice.

II.

Freddy wasn't home when he was needed.
He was packing boxes at UPS.
She made a tent of white sheets and pleaded
for him to camp in with her every night.

But he'd click on the same old *David Gilmour*
and shake down the Mass Pike with his brights on.
He'd talk to his lover a little more
on the phone but sometimes she wasn't home.

Her absence had Freddy a little stumped.
She started out just sniffing a few bumps.
She ran out of cash in need of long lines.
Then she learned that it is cheaper by the pipe.

Her father worked at the ol GM plant.
He had almost put in his thirty years.
She liked *David Coverdale, Bowie, Styx,*
Cheap Trick, Journey, and even *Bon Jovi.*

Close enough. So when her husband left her
and her son to get their first jobs ever
she went on a hunt for another man,
and chose for her son to learn self-defense.

Freddy was the sexiest Sensai she had
ever seen: curly long hair, a moustache—
David Coverdale in a Kempo jumper.
Freddy seemed smooth, parental, and easy.

IV.

Too easy. There was one big thing missing
from that waterbed. Sex and he was ready.
She wrapped him with her tongue and tied him up.
It only took a weekend to make him

jump when she said jump, come when she said come.
In another month he wrote four hundred
poems to her love or about his love
for her. He was ready to take the plunge.

It was time for him to move out the house.
To build a life and have kids with this woman.
Some said slow down pal she's just your first girl.
Fred said she's the greatest girl in the world.

V

Freddy had opened up his own Kempo
Karate school under the auspices
and namesake of his Sensai Mr. Hu.
Mr. Hu was quite generous with his name.

Freddy could put it on his welcome sign
and get one free master lesson each month
in exchange for a master extortion
that wouldn't come to fruition for years.

For now Freddy had about forty kids,
Yellow belts, brown ones, and some black ones too.
He did birthday parties on the weekends
for extra cash. He was trusted with youth.

VI.

The picture disks and tickets took their toll
but Fred really wanted to buy a house
to fill with his dreams and rooms full of kids.
So she co-signed the dotted line with him.

The house was theirs. Marriage and kids on hold.
The house had previously been foreclosed.
Walls with unrepeatable graffiti
stains on the rugs that your kids shouldn't see.

Freddy went and got a line of credit.
Freddy was soon riding shiny red toys.
In a month Freddy had knocked down all the walls
and made a master bedroom for his queen.

VII.

First it was a cough, then it was a wheeze.
She got to the point where she couldn't breathe.
She lost her job before she lost her breath.
Fred didn't know she was smoking to death.

Freddy begged her to go to the doctor
but she didn't have any way to pay.
Her parents had all but forgotten her.
Freddy said don't worry I will pay your way.

She went to the doctor with Fred's blank check.
She said he said she had emphysema.
Freddy cried all night, his pillow was wet.
And why shouldn't have Freddy believed her?

VIII.

The treatment's going to cost a few grand
each month she said with water in her eye.
Freddy grabbed her hand with both of his hands.
Freddy Sapienza won't let you die!

Freddy booked for birthdays every weekend.
Freddy sold his disks at **KISS** conventions.
Freddy borrowed from anyone who would lend.
Who could quibble with Freddy's intensions?

He put a signed checked under a magnet
on the fridge to kick off every month,
take extra for food, mortgage, don't forget.
I'll try to be home for dinner for once.

IX.

She moved to the guest room so he could sleep.
My coughing must be driving you crazy.
Freddy didn't know why the room smelled so sweet,
nor why the window panes were so hazy.

Fred worked harder than any man alive.
He packed at UPS, came home by three,
slept until noon, and finished school at five.
Flew like a butterfly, stung like a bee.

For the woman he wanted for a wife,
for the woman he wanted to marry.
The woman he wanted to bear his child
even if Freddy had to carry it.

X.

Soon a blank check wasn't even enough.
By mid-month she'd still be high but also dry.
That's when things really started to get rough.
That's when she decided to cross the line.

She made big tips at the *Foxy Lady*.
She made and did even more after hours.
Lost a lot of weight. Her face was caving.
She was no longer offended when called a whore

as long as she had more money for crack.
She began sleeping the same hours as Fred.
Fred said I finally have my lover back.
She stays up all night to sleep in my bed.

XI.

She emptied her bowels on so many planes,
then fully cleaned the glove so many times,
so just once she left the washing behind;
with eyes closed, she swallowed the glove again.

When she walked off the plane she looked the same
as always, you'd never know she was a crime.
She went to a phone, she put in a dime,
called us up, and to pick her up we came.

We'd sent the cash for this gal months ago
and were anxious for her to shit the glove
on our floor, razor it, then watch the glow!
But nothing followed our tugs and shoves.

XII.

One morning the school buses swarmed, big bees
around the school across her new friend's street.
To her and her friends it was just white noise,
as were the megaphones of screaming heat.

A felony slapped her across the face.
She was busted but she didn't care.
This was one open and shut case
but Freddy showed up and paid all the bail.

She was definitely going away.
The only question was where and how long.
We were only watching the school kids play.
She didn't know she had done something wrong.

XIII.

After mourning Fred thought he was free.
Then four guys in suits showed up at his door.
Very politely, they asked for the keys.
Freddy wouldn't be living there no more.

He hadn't paid the mortgage in two years?
He had maxed out all his credit cards?
Freddy couldn't hold back a head of tears.
Getting out of this was going to be hard.

Freddy those checks never saw a doctor.
O Freddy the mortgage was never paid.
Her side said Freddy never talked to her.
Freddy dropped his knees and began to pray.

XIV.

I hated you before you hated me
Freddy screamed at his ex-girl's photograph.
Then he threw it against the wall and laughed
so hard he cried so hard he couldn't see.

Smashed! Just as you always used to be!
I put up with you for six and a half
Years. You were the biggest pain in the ass.
Look at you now, you've fallen to pieces.

You couldn't put yourself back together
if you tried. I'll pick you up in one sweep
and hold you just as when we were lovers.
I can't believe you have done this to me.

XV.

Wanna go out on a date? I don't have
a cent to my name, my girl is in jail,
and we will have to split the bill in half.
At any moment there's a chance I'll wail

about the fact my dreams are down the drain,
my house is gone, my car's a wreck, my head
hurts so much I may be going insane.
I want to go back to my waterbed!

Those lines scared away most every female
except Vanessa. She had been burned too,
her soon to be ex-husband spent her dreams.
She had a few kids and wasn't a fool.

XVI.

Her little Jonathan loved his mother,
loved *Star Wars*, loved his *Legos*, loved his bike.
Her teenage girl though, wouldn't even talk
to Vanessa or acknowledge Freddy.

Vanessa had a great smile, great body,
a sense of humor and a cackle laugh
that could turn into a I don't take no shit
from anyone I don't think I will like.

Freddy seemed weathered and wise, good with kids,
in need, and pretty cute in his own way.
Freddy said to himself I could love her.
Vanessa said this one I really like.

XVII.

Standing tall, clean, white, black topped, and phallic;
Nobska light can't be moved by wind or storm,
which is why this is the place that they picked
to wed, to let ferrys, gaelic faeries swarm

around their perfect day.   Slow boats slow clouds
in and above the bay, our hair ribbons
in a score on the hill, a quiet loud
thrill that no mortal could have written.

Vannessa's dress hand made from Chinese silk
that Freddy's best man's wife bought in China.
Arms full of flowers that can never wilt.
No place, no day, no wife that could be finer.

XVIII.

He held a string tight and got on his knees.
Flying high above the harbor happier
than Red Sox fans screaming on the ferries,
than the herring gull or your flag flapping.

Freddy said his head took off like a kite.
He saw all of his people below him.
Beside himself, from inside a new life.
Like sandbags, tears of joy helped him descend.

His mother cried, Freddy's friends all cried too,
Vanessa is someone who you deserve.
Vanessa's kin also thought Freddy someone who
would be great for her, who would calm her nerves.

XIX.

A Celtic staff was raised upon the hill
and an array of ribbons was brought forth.
Earth and sky, goddess and god, were all spilled
from the staff. The ribbons glowed like a torch.

The red for love, passion, and strength.
The green for health, prosperity, fertility.
White for spirituality, peace and length.
Brown was for home, healing, and the earth.

There was light blue; patience, understanding.
Dark blue, ocean-like for a safe journey.
Purple for progress and all it demands.
Orange for kindness, yellow confidence.

XX.

I vow you the first cut of my meat
followed by the first sip of my wine.
I promise you that I will never leave,
I am all yours until the end of time.

From this day it shall be your name I cry
out in the night, and your dreams I follow.
Each morning I will smile into your eyes,
I am here to shield you from all sorrow.

Nor shall any grievous word be spoken
for our marriage is sacred between us.
Love is too strong for it to be broken
You I cherish through the next life and this.

XXI.

In less than a year after the wedding
Her ex-husband met another woman.
He wanted to move to her house in Maine.
He also wanted to bring the children.

He and Vanessa had joint custody.
If he left he would be breaking the law.
She said I want both my kids close to me,
I'll never let you take them very far.

He said we'll have to hash this out in court.
She said you're crazy, you don't have a chance!
They both know this was going to hurt.
They each hung up on the phone with trembling hands.

XXII.

Jonathan don't forget what I told you
as he prepped the boy for the witness stand.
Thus far the trial was going quite smooth,
Vanessa was the mother and the man

who was both making and baking bread,
who fed, clothed, loved and drove the boy to school.
The lawyer says we are fine, Freddy said.
Let's not do anything to lose our cool.

Her ex had to come up with something fast
or he would have to leave his son behind.
He played the only card he thought he had.
The guy knew he was running out of time.

XXIII.

He told lil Johnny she'd take him away,
so there was only one thing he could do.
Johnny would have to take the stand and say
your mother did terrible things to you.

I love my mommy, she's not mean to me.
O lil Johnny you just don't understand.
Everything will be all right, you will see.
You can do this big boy, I know you can!

Johnny thought he wasn't supposed to lie.
Johnny also knew to obey his dad.
You should have seen the face on that lil guy,
this is enough to drive anyone mad.

XXIV.

The case started to look open and shut.
Jurors were ready to call it a day.
It was clear that Vanessa was worthy, but
they didn't know what Johnny was about to say.

The last thing to do is hear from the child.
The judge asked Johnny to raise his right hand
and tell nothing but the truth while
you answer questions up here on the stand.

Jonathan is there any reason why
you shouldn't stay in the state with your mom?
My mother beats me and drinks all the time.
In an instant Vanessa's case was gone.

XXV.

Vanessa couldn't believe what she heard.
She hardly drank and wouldn't touch her son!
He knew what he was saying was absurd,
she started to feel her life come undone.

Her lawyer said this is a tough appeal,
Maine is only a couple of hours away.
How could you say that! This is such a steal.
I can't believe it turned out this way.

Let me take you home, to lie on the couch.
Everything will be alright in the end.
I will talk to Jonathan, he will vouch
for you, he will be in our arms once again.

XXVI.

Freddy drove her back home, you get some rest
love, this has been the longest day ever.
He rubbed her back on the couch but the stress
made it impossible to relax her.

Let me run to get your favorite take out.
You haven't eaten anything all day.
I'll put on a show, you lie on the couch.
We can hold each other all night, okay?

She was out like a light when he got home.
He let her be while he ate his sandwich.
Picked her up to carry her to their room.
Her eyes were wide open, she had gone stiff.

XXVII.

Freddy Sapienza keeps on moving.
He's met another girl and is grooving
with her and her three pretty little girls.
Freddy has his wounds and she has hers.

They build a cautious love but one that burns
with affection, empathy, true words,
passion, and now a lifelong commitment.
Bad dreams and nightmares are largely past them.

I am taking it one step at a time,
Freddy keeps saying. She says, so am I.
There are no other ends to things like this.
The only way to live is to love.

ABOUT THE AUTHOR

KEVIN GALLAGHER is a poet, publisher, and political economist living in Boston, Massachusetts with his wife, Kelly, kids Theo and Estelle, and dog Rexroth. His recent books are *Loom* and *And Yet it Moves*. Gallagher edits *spoKe*, a Boston-area journal of poetry and poetics. He works as a professor of global development policy at Boston University.

FOR THE FULL DOS MADRES PRESS CATALOG:
www.dosmadres.com